HOSTAGES

Yussef El Guindi

I0139969

BROADWAY PLAY PUBLISHING INC
New York
www.broadwayplaypublishing.com
info@broadwayplaypublishing.com

DEDICATION

For David Ball and Arthur Ballet

HOSTAGES was first produced at Duke University opening in April 1988. The cast and director were as follows:

MEADOWS ....Jack Young
TED... Simon Billig
GUARD...Sara Cordelia Wrenn

Director .... David Ball

HOSTAGES was produced at A C T (San Francisco) Plays in Progress Series in December 1988. The cast and director were as follows:

MEADOWS ....Rick Hamilton
TED..Alan Kopischke
GUARD...Deborah Hecht

Director .... Anna Deavere Smith

HOSTAGES was produced at Miscreant Theatre in January 2010. The cast and director were as follows:

MEADOWS .... Jacob Knoll
TED...Jeff Barry
GUARD... Peter Macklin

Director ....Jack Young

HOSTAGES was produced at iTheatre Collaborative (Christopher Haines, Artistic Director) opening in May 2016. The cast and director were as follows:

MEADOWS .... Todd Michael Isaac
TED.. Mike Traylor
GUARD...Max Cano

Director.. Charles St Clair

HOSTAGES was produced by Radial Theater Project at 18th & Union in Seattle (David Gassner, Producing Director) opening on 19 October 2018. The cast and creative contributors were:

MEADOWS ....Nik Doner
TED.. Sam Hagen
GUARD.. Yusef Mahmoud

Director.. David Gassner
Stage manager.. Emma Hagerman
Lighting design .... Angelo Dometri
Costume design...Julia Evanovich
Props design.. Amy LaZerte
Sound design.. Evan Mosher

ACKNOWLEDGMENTS

My thanks to David Ball for first championing this play and producing it at Duke University in 1988. To the late Arthur Ballet for bringing it to A C T's Plays in Progress Series where it was directed that same year by aspiring writer and performer Anna Deavere Smith. To Casey Childs for bringing Duke's production to Primary Stages. To Jack Young and the folks at Miscreant Theatre (Jeff Barry and Jacob Knoll) for resurrecting and staging this play after a twenty-two-year dormancy. To Christopher Haines for similarly extending the life of this play by staging it at his theater in Arizona, and to Charles St Clair for directing it at that venue. And finally to David Gassner and 18th and Union in Seattle for staging the play.

Note about acknowledging cast and creative contributors: I was not able to track down the behind-the-scenes creative contributors on any but the last, most recent production here in my hometown of Seattle. My apologies to those people. Though I believe Greg Carter was the very first stage manager at the Duke University premiere production.

CHARACTERS & SETTING

MEADOWS, *age range: anywhere from mid 30s to late 40s*
TED, *age-range: anywhere from mid 30s to early 50s*
GUARD, *age range: anywhere from early 20s to mid 30s*

Time: Could be the present

An undisclosed location

Scene 1:
The tactile dome

(TED *and* MEADOWS *are blindfolded, dressed in track-suits and chained—their hands tied behind their backs—to the two ends of a radiator. Dim lighting. Silence.*)

MEADOWS: Well, anyway…it's a step in the right direction. *(Slight beat)* It's not first class… But, after a month and a half in a broom closet, this feels great. *(Slight beat)* Yay, spring's arrived. —Feels like. —A somewhat darkish spring. They couldn't have knotted this blindfold any tighter, the little shits. I'd love to see their mothers in my position. But…at least we get to stretch our legs a bit. *(Slight beat)* "Bit" being the operative word. *(Slight beat)* Still, count your blessings. And company no less. Those pricks are showing definite strains of humanity. What's next? Velvet-lined chains? Cushions? Muzak? *(Slight beat)* Ted?

TED: *(Slight beat)* Yes?

MEADOWS: It's been months since I've tried to be… well—funny might be stretching it, but… they say humor's meant to be liberating. Do you know any jokes?

TED: *(Slight beat)* I can't think of any at the moment.

MEADOWS: *(Slight beat)* Ted?

TED: What?

MEADOWS: Look…do you mind…? Would you mind if I, um…if I made sure you're—here.

TED: …

MEADOWS: Of course you're here. I know you're *here.*
I can hear you breathing. And a very nice rhythm
you've got going there. You don't know how good it is
to hear someone else *(Laughing)* breathing around here.
(Slight beat) But for all I know you could be coming in
over some really good loudspeakers or something. I
mean—I know you're *here,* I can smell you. And a very
nice smell you have. I mean it. Your smell, honestly,
your smell to me, considering you're not a talkative
person is of great comfort. Like having a compass…
Pointing…pointing towards another real live human
being. In the flesh. *(Slight beat)* After a month and a
half…Ted? …Ted?

TED: I'm here.

MEADOWS: Would you talk to me? Please?

TED: I'm sorry, yes.

MEADOWS: Would you mind if we, er…

(Slight beat)

TED: What?

MEADOWS: Played footsy. For a sec. It would help.
(Slight beat) It might help.

TED: Yes.

MEADOWS: Touch base? Find, you know—

TED: I understand.

MEADOWS: each other, physically. I'm feeling a little
claustrophobic knowing there's someone else in the
room and not knowing where he is.

TED: I'm here.

MEADOWS: I *know.* I know that, Ted. I feel you vibrating
the radiator. Only I'm not sure it's not me vibrating
the radiator. I could be having this conversation all

by myself. I've had many heart-to-hearts with myself these past months in that closet. If we could just touch base with our legs, with a—tap or something.

TED: Yes, sure.

MEADOWS: A little—

TED: I'm moving towards you.

(TED *shifts his body around the radiator to get nearer to* MEADOWS.)

MEADOWS: Because I can't go on listening to a voice that could well be mine.

TED: I'm here. (*He extends his leg.*)

MEADOWS: Christ, Ted, I *know* that.

TED: No, no, I'm here. I've got my leg out.

MEADOWS: Where?

TED: Shift yourself around.

(MEADOWS *shifts himself. Both* MEADOWS *and* TED *have awkwardly twisted their torsos so that their legs can meet in the middle.*)

MEADOWS: Where are you?

TED: Extend your leg.

(MEADOWS *and* TED *grope with their legs. They touch for a moment but then lose each other.*)

TED: I had you.

MEADOWS: Try again.

(MEADOWS's *and* TED's *legs touch again.*)

MEADOWS: There—there you are. Alright.

TED: Okay?

MEADOWS: Yes. Yes. (*He clamps his leg more firmly on top of* TED's.) Thank you. —Thank you. (*Slight beat*) Is this alright?

TED: Fine... You could ease up a little.

MEADOWS: Sorry.

TED: It's okay. Just—

MEADOWS: Did I come down too hard?

TED: It's fine.

MEADOWS: Is this better?

TED: Yes. Good.

MEADOWS: Just for a moment... Do you mind?

TED: Why should I?

MEADOWS: It makes all the difference.

TED: Happy to help.

(Beat)

MEADOWS: I'm sorry they got you. *(Slight beat)* Last person I expected to see with me. *(Slight beat)* No rhyme or reason, huh? *(He laughs.)*

TED: What?

MEADOWS: Oh...I was about to say...welcome aboard. *(Slight beat)* It doesn't sound right, does it: "welcome aboard". *(Slight beat)* Welcome aboard anyway.

(Beat. Fade to blackout.)

Scene 2:
The person next to me

(MEADOWS and TED are positioned as before: MEADOW's leg on top of TED's. Silence)

MEADOWS: Would you mind if you took off your left shoe? *(Slight beat)* Ted?

TED: Why?

MEADOWS: Why do I want you to take off your left shoe? I'll tell you why. I think it's the left foot. The big toe on your left foot. Where the scar is? You do have a scar—or, a scab? On the big toe of your left foot?

TED: ...

MEADOWS: Ted?

TED: What are you talking about?

MEADOWS: Could you just tell me.

TED: What about it?

MEADOWS: You have one, right?

TED: Yes.

MEADOWS: Left foot? ...Left foot?

TED: *Yes.*

MEADOWS: I remember your scar from the beach. —Do you remember that outing? Faculty get together with the students. —Fraternizing with the students in a relaxed atmosphere. What's-his-name's bright idea. Bombs fell around the time we got on a first name basis. I noticed your scar for some reason. *(Slight beat)* I suppose you want to know why I...I need to feel for that scar right now. *(Slight beat)* Ted, listen to me... *(Almost a whisper)* Listen... *(He removes his leg from Ted's.)* What did I just do?

TED: ...

MEADOWS: Ted?

TED: What?

MEADOWS: Did you feel that?

TED: ...

MEADOWS: You didn't feel that?

TED: Feel what?

MEADOWS: Feel me do anything.

TED: You lifted your leg.

MEADOWS: You felt it?

TED: You want to tell me what's going on?

(MEADOWS *drapes his leg back over* TED's.)

MEADOWS: Now?

TED: …

MEADOWS: Answer me.

TED: I'd like to know what's going on.

MEADOWS: Is my leg over yours?

TED: Of course it is.

MEADOWS: That's all I want to know.

(Beat)

TED: You okay?

MEADOWS: Taking into account our condition, I'm hanging in there.

(Slight beat)

TED: What was all that business about my scar?

MEADOWS: You wouldn't let me feel it, would you?

TED: …

MEADOWS: I'll tell you why.

TED: It's not a request I usually get.

MEADOWS: It's not a fetish of mine either. I don't go feeling for scars out of pleasure, just so you know.

TED: I'm sure you don't.

MEADOWS: It's not what I do on Saturday nights. I've other ticks, scar hunting isn't one of them.

TED: It's not why I asked. It's just… I've never been approached by someone who wants to feel my scar.

MEADOWS: I'm not usually in a situation where the need arises to feel for someone's scar.

(Beat)

TED: So why do you want to feel it?

MEADOWS: I'll tell you why.

(Slight beat)

TED: I suppose after a month and a half, you, er… There's a need to… It's the little things you remember?

MEADOWS: That's not it.

TED: Or—like—with the leg business?

MEADOWS: No.

TED: Needing to make sure? Touch base?

MEADOWS: No no, that's not it.

TED: Isolation will do that to you.

MEADOWS: This isn't about reassuring myself emotionally. I'm not trying to feel your scar to— whatever. I'm not a…I'm not a pervert, in case you're—

TED: What? No. I didn't think that. That's the last thing I thought.

MEADOWS: Well I'd wonder if *I* had a scar and you asked to touch it. For no other reason than you needed—because you needed to. That *would* be weird.

TED: I'm not worried on that account.

MEADOWS: Well I would be.

(Slight beat)

TED: Do you want to tell me why you want to feel my scar?

MEADOWS: I'm not absolutely sure you're the person next to me. *(Slight beat)* I can't remember how you smell...I never made a note of how you smell. It crossed my mind I may be smelling someone else. *(Slight beat)* Did you ever make a note of how *I* smell? Ted? Not without deodorants and half a bottle of cologne you haven't. It occurred to me... *(Slight beat)* It occurred to me they're playing a game... They took me out of the closet to play this game where I'm led to believe Ted Burrows is next to me... I swear I heard someone giggle.

TED: You shouldn't do that.

MEADOWS: How do you know it's my leg?

TED: I'm talking to you aren't I?

MEADOWS: Your voice could be coming through a really good speaker. It's amazing what they can do with sound these days. You could be in another room.

TED: Stop it. It doesn't make any of this easier.

MEADOWS: How do you know that's my leg? *(He moves his leg.)*

TED: I felt you move it.

(MEADOWS shakes his leg over TED's.)

TED: You're jiggling it about.

MEADOWS: ...

TED: You were jiggling it about, right?

MEADOWS: What if they're imitating everything I do?

(TED moves his leg.)

TED: Feel that?

MEADOWS: I can't tell. My leg's gone numb.

(TED comes down hard on MEADOWS's leg.)

TED: How about that?

MEADOWS: *(Winces)* That hurt.

TED: Good. You know it's me then.

(Beat)

MEADOWS: They could be imitating you.

TED: Medcalf:—

MEADOWS: It would help if you got my name right.

TED: You'll end up hurting yourself if you let your mind play games like that. Of course I'm next to you. Who else would be here? You hear me breathing don't you? I hear you.

MEADOWS: Again, the things you can do with great audio. Please don't bother to scream in my ear. There could be a hole in the wall. How do we know they didn't move their legs between the time we moved ours, and the time we got to responding?

TED: Why? *(Slight beat)* Why would they go to all that trouble?

MEADOWS: How should I know?

TED: To accomplish what?

MEADOWS: Amuse themselves? Joke around?

TED: We've been here for hours… That's a lot of patience just to play a joke on us.

MEADOWS: They're a patient people. *(Slight beat)* Didn't you ever wait around the corner for your sister to pass by so you could jump out? I'd wait for hours just to scare her and get her to scream…I tell you I heard someone giggle.

TED: You're not helping yourself.

MEADOWS: It's possible, isn't it?

TED: And what if it is? If I'm not sitting next to you—

MEADOWS: Then someone besides me is next to you.

TED: I know who's next to me.

MEADOWS: How can you be sure?

TED: This is how.

(TED *comes down hard on* MEADOWS*'s leg.* MEADOWS *flinches.)*

TED: Want me to repeat that?

MEADOWS: Proves nothing.

(Beat)

TED: You sure you don't have a fetish? *(Slight beat)* It's not the end of the world if you do. I think we can agree, certain sectors of academia are a breeding ground for…unique fixations.

MEADOWS: It's not me who has a fetish.

TED: I'm sure you don't.

MEADOWS: It's not me with the fixation, Ted.

TED: I don't think you actually do, I was just—

MEADOWS: It's them who brought us here who have a problem worth looking into. They're the fucking perverts. They're the ones with the fetish. We're it. We're their horrible little fetish.

TED: I never meant to imply—

MEADOWS: Have you noticed how polite they are. Always saying "sorry." As if they couldn't help themselves. As if they had an uncontrollable fetish for abducting foreigners.

TED: I wouldn't call it a fetish.

MEADOWS: Nothing to do with politics. Nothing whatsoever to do with that. You can't say this is a politically motivated compulsion. It's something a lot seamier than politics. It's got to do with blood, Ted. Race.

TED: Stop.

MEADOWS: National character. It's genetic. A belief system so ingrained it's passed down through the genes.

TED: Seriously.

MEADOWS: *(Overlapping)* I've really come to believe that. You hear me?

TED: You're way off.

MEADOWS: Not you, I'm not addressing you, *him.*

(MEADOWS comes down hard on TED's leg. TED flinches, moves his leg away.)

MEADOWS: The little pervert beside me. Let's see if we can't flush them out.

TED: That was my leg you hit.

MEADOWS: The bastards are imitating us.

TED: You bruised my leg.

MEADOWS: Bruise him back.

TED: Medcalf.

MEADOWS: Kick him.

(MEADOWS comes down hard again.)

TED: Stop it.

(TED moves his leg further away.)

MEADOWS: That did it. Do you feel a leg? Mine moved his.

TED: For God's sake.

(Slight beat)

MEADOWS: History's littered with examples of their violent fascination with us. They're drawn to all things Western. Envy. Plain and simple. *(Slight beat; then:)* I could be wrong. It could be you. —It just makes sense though, given the way they think and act. Can't you feel them watching?

TED: I'm not taking my shoe off so you can feel for a damn scar. It's cold enough at night as it is. You'll just have to take my word it's me who's sitting beside you.

(Slight beat)

MEADOWS: Either way there's nothing we can do about it. —I just wanted to make sure. I don't like being the butt of someone's joke. It's bad enough being at the receiving end of someone's fetish.

TED: If you let this get to you? Like this? You'll end up going nuts. You'll get more stressed out, more paranoid. Things are bad enough as it is without—

MEADOWS: Paranoid? That's a redundant observation in these surroundings. Of course I'm fucking paranoid. I got abducted. That's pretty solid ground for being paranoid. That says I wasn't paranoid enough.

TED: If you feel my scar you'll say he has one.

MEADOWS: No: I don't think it's likely he'd have a scar on his left foot.

TED: He could have checked when he laced my shoe. Glued something resembling dead skin on his big toe. On the odd chance you'd become suspicious that it wasn't me next to you and wanted to check.

(Beat)

MEADOWS: I know you're trying to screw with me but that's not so implausible. I wouldn't put it past them. They're that devious.

TED: If they're playing this game, we'll find out eventually. They have to pee sometime.

(Beat)

MEADOWS: Move your leg over then.

(Slight beat)

TED: Whose leg are you talking about?

MEADOWS: His—for all it matters.

(Slight beat. TED *slides his leg next to* MEADOWS. MEADOWS *drapes his leg over* TED'S. *Slight beat. Fade to blackout.)*

Scene 3:
Lessons

(Same position as before… TED *tenses… He withdraws his leg and slides away from* MEADOWS.*)*

MEADOWS: What's going on?

TED: Um…

(Beat)

MEADOWS: Why'd you move?

TED: …

MEADOWS: Cramp?

TED: No.

MEADOWS: Need to stretch?

TED: I'm…alright.

MEADOWS: I day-dream when I feel like stretching… I imagine I'm walking somewhere. Through the woods. On the beach. Feeling the sand between my toes. Temporary solution but it works. Problem is, it's hard to keep it up. And when you come out of it—all this can feel even worse.

TED: I'm… That's not it.

(Beat)

MEADOWS: Astral projection would be ideal. Know anything about astral projection?

TED: No.

MEADOWS: Is it something I said? Your moving away?

TED: No... It's something I'm about to do.

MEADOWS: What are you about to do? ...Leave me?

TED: I have to... *(Beat)* There's a small question of...
bowel movements.

(Slight beat)

MEADOWS: What's stopping you?

TED: Thirty-seven years of toilet training... *(Adjust to the actor's age)* What do you do? When you have to...
When you can't hold it.

MEADOWS: I let go.

(Slight beat)

TED: Perhaps I should call out to them.

MEADOWS: They haven't answered the call of nature
since I've been here... There are set times when they
come in and attend to the coarser points of abduction.
Otherwise you go through a lot of red tape to take a
crap.

(Slight beat)

TED: When are they due in?

MEADOWS: How desperate are you?

TED: Matter of minutes.

MEADOWS: Forget it. Relax. I promise I won't raise a
stink if you don't. *(Amused by his own joke)* You should
have smelt my closet.

TED: *(Under his breath)* Christ.

MEADOWS: So much for you supporting their cause.

TED: What?

MEADOWS: It is a crap we're talking about? Not a piss?

TED: Both.

MEADOWS: *(Slight beat)* Like a toothache isn't it… Nothing else matters… Famine, war. The rights of unborn babies. Your discomfort, your pain: that's what counts. To hell with the rest. I learnt a lot from my first crap in these conditions. It set my priorities straight. I sat there for a day or so with the shit running down my legs, caking my skin—

TED: Could you please not—go into that?

MEADOWS:—before they came in and gave me something else to wear. You know what line kept running through my head? "These fragments I have shored against my ruins." —T S Eliot. You never know when your education will come in handy.

TED: …

MEADOWS: Shat yet?

TED: No.

MEADOWS: I suppose I'll know.

(TED tenses. Beat)

MEADOWS: Years of good, solid toilet training— civilized behavior: sabotaged.

TED: I wish you wouldn't.

MEADOWS: I'm trying to help. —I realize of all the people you'd least want to witness your incontinence, it's me. It's no secret we weren't buddies. But we're joined at the hip now, literally. Something nasty intruded into our lives. Their dating service paired us together. We're going to be intimates for who knows how long. No point in being precious about a shit. *(Slight beat)* It's all relative here. That's something you should get across in your political science class. The profoundest lessons are packed in the least likely moments. Hold a workshop where your students have to simulate these conditions. Before the day's through they'll gladly swap their ideals for a clean toilet seat and a roll of paper.

(TED *urinates, defecates. Silence*)

MEADOWS: I—gather you've passed with flying colors. From the... change of odor in the air. *(Slight beat)* Wasn't so difficult, was it? *(Slight beat)* A bit humiliating... But that passes. *(Slight beat)*

TED: Medcalf.

MEADOWS: It's Meadows. —What?

TED: About someone else sitting beside you.

MEADOWS: ...

TED: You're right.

MEADOWS: ...

TED: Smell it don't you? ...It wasn't me. —I faked it... I faked a call of nature to test your theory... Someone else in this room relieved himself.

MEADOWS: Ted.

TED: I was wrong.

MEADOWS: There's no shame in claiming your own shit.

TED: I called their bluff. Only they're not bluffing. They're taking this game very seriously.

MEADOWS: There's no need to be embarrassed. There's no room for embarrassment here.

TED: I'm serious. —You were right.

MEADOWS: *(Slight beat)* You're saying there's a person sitting beside me who went so far as to crap in his pants because he thought you were crapping in yours?

TED: Yup... Fanatics.

(Slight beat)

MEADOWS: Seriously, Ted. Just own up to it... They wouldn't go that far.

TED: No? Suicide missions aren't far?—You're the one who thinks they're a perverse bunch. —Defecation in the line of duty isn't far for a man who's willing to strap himself to explosives. Different set of priorities.

(Beat)

MEADOWS: You're fucking with me. —You're pulling my leg.

TED: You've been warned.

MEADOWS: You're just too embarrassed to admit you shat.

TED: There's someone else here. I can smell them.

MEADOWS: It's not funny, Ted. You shouldn't joke around like that.

TED: I'm not.

MEADOWS: It's a real possibility.

TED: I know. I flushed them out.

(Slight beat)

MEADOWS: If I find out you're jerking me around. If you're playing on my fears just to avoid owning up— I'll be really upset.

TED: If you didn't have those fears to begin with— people wouldn't play about with them, would they.

(Slight beat)

MEADOWS: You *are* pulling my leg.

TED: Would you strap yourself to explosives for a cause?

MEADOWS: ...

TED: There are those who would.

MEADOWS: Ted: did you or did you not relieve yourself?

TED: I've always wondered how it feels to be so committed. —So dedicated.

MEADOWS: Ted...please answer me...*Ted*?

(Slight Beat. Blackout)

Scene 4:
Open door

(Bright lights. The door is open. MEADOWS *and* TED *are unbound. Both men look at the open door. Beat)*

TED: Oversight?

MEADOWS: You think?

TED: It happens.

MEADOWS: True. True.

TED: People forget to switch off their stoves. The tap is left running... The door to the room you're holding two prisoners is left open...

(Beat)

MEADOWS: I heard our Air Force accidentally dropped a nuclear device over one of the states once... That must have been a slap-to-the-forehead moment.

TED: I bet. *(Slight beat)* A way out, you think?

MEADOWS: I'm not waltzing into a trap.

TED: You think it's a trap?

MEADOWS: Well look at it. They didn't just leave the door ajar. If it was slightly open, okay, maybe an accident; an oversight. But this? ...This is an invitation to a firing squad.

TED: Could be an honest mistake.

MEADOWS: Or an excuse to kill us. "Died while trying to escape."

TED: I don't think they need an excuse to do that.

MEADOWS: It's another one of their games.

TED: Why would they leave the door wide open?

MEADOWS: You tell me. You did your PhD on them.

(Beat)

TED: Huh… Well? …What do you think?

MEADOWS: I don't know… It's too risky. —Too easy.

TED: Testing us? Wanting to see if we'll be good little captives?

MEADOWS: Another one of their jokes. Bring the curtain down with a big laugh. A big finale.

TED: Or maybe they want us to escape. —A way out for them too… Maybe they made a deal.

MEADOWS: Wouldn't they tell us?—Why wouldn't they tell us if they'd made a deal—with our government?— No. It's more of their games. I can feel it. I don't trust them for a second.

TED: So? …What do you suggest? *(Beat. He walks to another position to see if he can get a better look at what's outside.)* We could stick our heads out… See what's going on.

(Slight beat)

MEADOWS: Go for it. I'll hold down the fort.

(TED looks at MEADOWS.)

We can't both stick our heads out. I'll do it if you want. It'll just look silly if we both stick our heads out. —A question of dignity. I'd like to maintain *some* dignity in front of them should they be watching. *(Slight beat)*

Little bastards. Leaving the door wide open like that.
What are they playing at?

(TED *approaches the door. Beat. He closes the door...
Blackout.)*

Scene 5:
The temptations of Winnie-The-Pooh

(Bright lights. Two deck chairs. Several books. TED *is seated
reading. He's alone in the room. Silence. Sound of a toilet
flushing. When the sound dies down* MEADOWS *emerges
from behind a curtain.)*

MEADOWS: We are still receiving our monthly checks,
don't you think? The university wouldn't just stop
paying us, would they?

TED: *(Still reading)* I have no idea.

MEADOWS: I'll sue if they have. Breach of contract.

TED: How is it breach of contract?

MEADOWS: They have to count this as—sick leave or
something. Or—combat pay even.

TED: I'm not sure academics qualify for combat pay. In
or out of the classroom. As rowdy as they can get.

MEADOWS: Sick leave then. Through no fault of our
own we were taken by sickos. Made sick by their
sickness. Overcome by an infectious disease in combat
fatigues.

TED: Might be regarded as too broad an interpretation.

MEADOWS: What interpretation would you give our
situation?

TED: I haven't thought about it.

MEADOWS: It's not the money. I don't care about the
money. It would be nice, of course. But. It's the thought

of them casually crossing our names out. "No longer
with us. Address unknown. Stop all payments. Too
bad about Ted and Meadows, what's for dinner?" Ever
so casually: "what's for dinner?"

(TED *turns a page. Beat.* MEADOWS *crosses to stand behind*
TED.)

MEADOWS: The idea of being deleted like that doesn't
trouble you?

TED: …

MEADOWS: Firmly ensconced in the realm of political
theory, are we?

TED: …

MEADOWS: Feeling smug in our calmness?

TED: Medcalf.

MEADOWS: It must be so pleasant to live in your own
head all the time… I suppose the rent is cheap.

TED: I'd like to read.

MEADOWS: This must be especially humiliating for
you. Being here. Ted Burrows. Political activist.
Fighter for the oppressed, etc. Held hostage by the
people he once championed. Ironic. No? If irony felt
like a steel rod shoved up one's ass. (*He begins to circle
around the room.*) I mean…don't you think? When you
compare the set-up: your beliefs, what you stood for;
and—where you ended up: (*A gesture that takes in their
surroundings.*) the punchline. This. (*Slight beat*) A man
throws off the shackles of his mother country. Cries
sham on its foreign policy. Rails against imperialism;
screams about this and that injustice. He takes up the
banner of Byronic liberation. Crosses a continent and
an ocean and runs head on into…the real thing. Not
theory. Not academic-speak or conference palaver.
Not even cute brown people looking for help. No,

more like cute brown people ready to blow your
head off. Not grateful at all... Oops? *(Slight beat)* I'd
feel screwed... if I were in your shoes. I mean—me?
I just have the obvious to worry about. As long as I
keep from bouncing off these walls; and deal with the
obvious mental health issues that arise when a man
has been *kidnapped*—and lives with the threat of death
constantly, I'll be fine. I have a family to return to.
A country I love. A place where I can unashamedly
expose my wobbly pink stomach on sunny days. What
do you have?

TED: ...

MEADOWS: You can't return to your old beliefs now
can you. Your political mantras. —The high perch
from which you looked down on the rest of us
mildly centrist, political non-committals. Next to the
expression "Looking down your nose" they really
should have a picture of you by way of explanation.
All that has to be kind of—deceased at this point. If
you're honest with yourself. And guess who did them
in?

TED: *(Turns a page)* Killing time, are we?

MEADOWS: The oppressed... Your beloved,
downtrodden, "pauvre, pauvre." —They didn't quite...
well they didn't quite behave like they should've.
Which has to be—you know...disappointing. *(Slight
beat)* Don't get me wrong. I am trying to be empathetic.
I do have a stake in your well-being. If something's
gnawing at you, I'll know about it. We have no privacy
to let things fester here. Whatever our differences,
our getting out in one piece, our getting out at all—
depends on our being united. If something's gnawing
at you, I want to help. *(Slight beat)* You've been
dumped. Figuratively speaking. That has to be just—
eating away at you.

TED: And what's eating away at you?

MEADOWS: Nothing; I just told you. I'm only here for as long as they keep me. My old life's waiting for me. Yours has been turned on its head. Worse: you've been tarred and feathered by the people you supported.

TED: I don't see it that way.

MEADOWS: You don't want to face it, do you. Which I understand. I do denial of unpleasant truths all the time. But the facts remain. I wish you'd put down that book and talk to me.

TED: I wish you'd keep your empathy to yourself.

MEADOWS: If you're so sympathetic with those bastards how come you're here?

TED: What's the end goal of all this "concern" you're showing?

MEADOWS: Care and comfort—for you, obviously. Plus I'm just trying to clear the air between us.

TED: Is that what you're doing.

MEADOWS: I'd love to know what keeps you from calling their mothers horrible names. While holding a grudge against me for wishing to see the people who put me here die a painful death.

TED: Listen to me, Medcalf.

MEADOWS: *It's: Meadows.* For the umpteenth fucking time.

TED: Here's the thing…I don't want you to feel even more abandoned, but, honestly? I don't have the energy, or, frankly, the emotional investment in you to hold any kind of grudge. And if the point of your "empathy" is to have me beat myself up because what I believed in may have led to my capture, I wouldn't hold your breath. I wouldn't jerk off on that whole "schadenfreude" thing, which you're clearly doing. This war, the people I was supposedly trying to help, did not emerge full blown from either of our heads. We are not—we are barely bit players in their struggle. What's happened to us takes nothing away from the real grievances they still have. Their struggle remains a just one, even if we're now counted among its casualties; or because a gang of... *(He's about to say "thugs".)* ...idiots among them thought they could change things by abducting us. My only regret is that now *we've* become part of the problem.

MEADOWS: Wow.

TED: Yes. Actually.

MEADOWS: Just wow.

TED: Their stupid tactics doesn't mean they don't still have a righteous cause. I just wish they would have thought things through before acting like thugs.

MEADOWS: When you can say all that with a straight face. When you can sit there and reel off a political manifesto like it's a Christmas carol. Or act like you're their PR person, even after what's happened to us... What did you cuddle up to at night before this? A bust of Karl Marx? A blow-up doll of Pol Pot?

TED: If you're really concerned with my well-being, you could do something very concrete right here and now that would make a huge difference to me.

MEADOWS: What would that be?

TED: Shut up. You could in fact just shut up. For a while. A few long whiles strung together. Preferably.

(TED goes back to reading. Beat)

MEADOWS: Honestly...Ted...deep down—heart of hearts...you never expected this...I don't mean to keep pressing the point—

TED: *(Turning the page, under his breath)* Oh but you do.

MEADOWS: You truly believed—your politics—would somehow exempt you. You never imagined your character—you—politically nuanced you—would be reduced to your passport. Your country of origin. Like the rest of us. You actually thought your writings, your political credentials would somehow protect you. *(Perhaps he draws closer to* TED. *Or not)* Did you think they'd care? About something as wishy-washy as your sympathies? It doesn't translate, professor. There's no value. There's no appreciation for something as layered as "where you stand." Your beliefs, your wonderfully commendable political acumen has about as much impact around here, has less value, than a roll of toilet paper. *(Slight beat)* All we are, what we amount to to them are bargaining chips. We're currency. If the market collapses on the exchange rate for hostages, and our hosts with the righteous cause find they can't buy shit for two professors, we'll go where all worthless currency goes. Into the shredder. *(Slight beat)* Oh I've been burned. No doubt about it. Burned and possibly dumped. *(Using the tail of his shirt—or a book perhaps—he fans himself as he walks to another part of the room.)* You: you've been betrayed. *(Slight beat)* It's not that I'm trying to knock you…much. You're welcome to your illusions like the rest of us. It just ticks me off to think we're not on the same page. Maybe not even on the same side. Which is just…mind-blowing to me.

(Slight beat)

TED: Why did you come to this country?

MEADOWS: What?

TED: You've hated everything about this place since the moment you arrived. In the faculty meetings: the number of times you complained, on and on. There must have been other jobs. You could have stayed home. Why did you come here?

(Beat)

MEADOWS: I...I wanted an affair.

(Slight beat)

TED: I didn't catch that.

(Slight beat)

MEADOWS: I said I wanted an affair.

TED: An affair?

MEADOWS: Yes. The adulterous sort?—I wanted to cheat on my wife... It's not like being honest will cost me anything here...I'd...married young...I thought if I came here I could work out a few...personal issues— in the privacy of a foreign country. Out of sight out of mind? —Silly—fantasies. You know: exotic locale. Different customs. Freeing you up to... you know.

TED: ...

MEADOWS: That sort of thing... Not ashamed to admit it now, however it makes me look. And doing it all free of guilt. It's not as bad if it happens in a foreign country. You don't feel quite as... accountable. When you're surrounded by familiar things, your family, friends, then yes: guilt. But in a foreign country. It might as well be happening to another person. You're not quite the you that everyone knows— who's expected to behave in a certain way. Not as responsible. Not as exposed...God knows I tried...I just couldn't find anyone to cheat with. *(Slight beat)* I must've read the wrong brochure.

(Slight beat)

TED: I see.

MEADOWS: You see how honest I am.

TED: I do.

MEADOWS: It's a pity you can't show me the same courtesy.

TED: ...

MEADOWS: I suppose you find that laughable. A Westerner goes abroad to find fleshy comfort in the arms of a desperate "Third World" woman. Hideously exploitative. Typical, horrible. A just punishment for the sins of his errant dick.

TED: You're saying it. Not me.

MEADOWS: It's like talking to a government bureaucrat with you. Words, but—nothing really there. A compendium of dry statements but—kinda short on that whole humanity thing. *(Slight beat)* Anyway. That's how I ended up as a guest here. *(He lifts the curtain and looks in.)* In these first class accommodations... Then again...we should be grateful for small comforts. *(He exits into the room, speaking:)* At least it's a toilet and not a bucket. Let us praise the gifts of small conveniences.

(TED checks to see MEADOWS has left. He hears MEADOWS clearing his throat and spitting. The sound of water running. TED looks at the chair beside him. On impulse he lifts the rung of the deck chair from its groove and places it on the floor. It remains standing, precariously so. He returns to his book. MEADOWS speaks from offstage:)

MEADOWS: And: to add insult to injury: *(Emerging from behind the curtain, wiping his face.)* They give us "Winnie-The-Pooh Cook Book" to read... It boggles the mind to think they might have used that book to cook themselves something... Gun-toting fanatics pouring over the recipe for "Poohanpiglet Pancakes". Where do you go with a thought like that?

TED: It's one way to learn English.

MEADOWS: Does that book really demand all your concentration? Do you really want to die with the ingredients of Pea-Bean Alphabet soup on your mind?

(TED *flips through the pages.*)

TED: I haven't gotten to that recipe yet.

MEADOWS: Well don't spoil it by jumping to the end. Though, spoiler alert: the recipe demands a shit load of peas and beans. I'll leave just how much as a surprise. (*He stands directly behind* TED, *leaning on the back of his deck chair. Beat*) You really do have all the appeal of a government bureaucrat... Stainless steel paper clip holding yourself together. (*Slight beat*) And when it comes to bureaucrats, I have found...you either accept their life-sapping dullness, and deal with them, or: if you haven't the patience, and you can't escape them... you shrug off decorum and express exactly how you feel.

(MEADOWS *lifts the rung off its groove. The chair and* TED *collapse. Beat*)

MEADOWS: I think I did that on purpose. —In the interest of letting off steam. In the long run—I think it was the right move. For both of us. Getting things off our chest; and not letting them fester. You don't want small irritants to build up and become a bigger problem later on. Yeah?—Are you okay?

(MEADOWS *helps* TED *get up. They right the chair.* TED *sits. While doing this they speak:*)

TED: Fine.

MEADOWS: Sure?

TED: Nothing damaged.

MEADOWS: Sorry. Sorry about that.

TED: Don't sweat it. I get it. Could you pass me the book?

(MEADOWS *passes* TED *the book.*)

MEADOWS: Really. I'm…very sorry. —No hard feelings, yeah? I promise—. Well I shouldn't promise but…that was probably it. As far as outbursts. For a very long time.

TED: You know what…it's okay. I'll recover.

MEADOWS: Good… Good… Well…I feel better… In fact—I think I'll join you. (*He picks a book from the pile.*) Nothing like a good read to while away the months… *The Count Of Monte Cristo.* Subtle bastards aren't they.

(MEADOWS *sits in the chair. It collapses, along with* MEADOWS. TED *turns to look.* MEADOWS *looks at* TED… TED *goes back to his book. He smiles. He turns a page. Fade to black.*)

Scene 6:
The hug

(MEADOWS *and* TED *face each other.*)

MEADOWS: I hate to ask. But…I do think—um. I think I'd like to, er… Yeah. —Basically.

TED: The, er—?

MEADOWS: Yeah. Follow through. With that…request.

(*Slight beat*)

TED: You mean—?

MEADOWS: Yes. That… Yeah.

TED: Okay. (*Shrugs*) Sure. —Now?

MEADOWS: I think so. (*Nods his head to indicate he's in agreement with his expressed need.*)

TED: Why not. Sure.

MEADOWS: I hate to ask but I'm—having—a moment here. Otherwise known as a—well—a moment. Making ends—the ends— meet in a… *(Makes hand gestures indicating two things trying to flow towards each other.)* Actually, fuck that. I could just use a big, thumping, you know—with all the trimmings.

TED: *(Not enthused)* Of course; of course, yes.

MEADOWS: I wouldn't ask if it wasn't absolutely… I'm not sure why—suddenly—it's necessary, all of a sudden. But—there it is.

TED: I understand.

MEADOWS: You know, a big… *(Mimes a hug)* …one of those things. As a favor.

TED: It's not—. Don't call it that. Nothing to do with favors.

MEADOWS: I'm not implying that—you're not—you know, instinctively—forthcoming in matters of—. Honestly: —I think underneath that rough exterior of yours—you have a natural, well-spring of… feeling.

TED: Um… I do.

MEADOWS: Good, because—I just want to make sure you don't think I'm—saying that—trying to get a hug from you is like—pulling teeth or anything.

TED: I didn't think you were—saying that.

MEADOWS: Because I'm not.

TED: You're asking for a perfectly normal—thing; it's fine. It's not outside my wheelhouse, believe it or not.

MEADOWS: I know it's not. Oh I know it's not. I wouldn't have asked if I thought it was. Like I said, I sense underneath it all you're a very—warm—individual.

TED: I am.

MEADOWS: I agree. You dig far enough and I bet you'd find the heart of a cuddle bunny.

TED: *(Slight beat)* I wouldn't go that far.

MEADOWS: Maybe not "cuddle bunny", but: in the same family.

TED: I think your request is—very healthy. *(Rolls his eyes; to himself)* "Healthy".

MEADOWS: What?

TED: Stupid thing to say.

MEADOWS: I don't think it is. I don't think so.

(Slight beat)

TED: You're not feeling well?

MEADOWS: Ted… *(Slight beat)* I'm not asking for medical attention. I just want a little physical contact. And it has nothing to do with sex, I hope that's clear.

TED: No, I understand. Not a problem… How will we do this then?

(Slight beat)

MEADOWS: Well… the way I hear it's done—we face each other… we extend our arms wide. We open them up. We step towards each other. We glue each other around the chest area for a couple of moments, wrapping our arms around each other's back. And hold the position… Beyond that, I can't predict. *(Slight beat)* I see it done in the movies all the time. A cliche, I grant you, but it never seems to get old.

TED: You're not being fair.

MEADOWS: I wish I hadn't asked.

TED: I'm willing.

MEADOWS: Your enthusiasm is killing me.

TED: Give me a moment. You're not the most huggable person in the world. I was caught off guard, that's all. *(Slight beat)* I like being hugged. I like hugging. I've done it many times before, with many people, just not with you. That's all.

MEADOWS: I'm not asking you to sleep with me.

TED: You have an endless talent for being an ass, you know that? *(Slight beat)* Alright. *(He extends his arms.)* Come on then. Let's do it.

(Beat. MEADOWS doesn't move.)

MEADOWS: *(To himself)* Like trying to hug a fucking syringe.

TED: *(He lowers his arms.)* I didn't catch that.

MEADOWS: The moment's passed. Good job.

TED: A syringe? Is that what you said? —Well God knows what you might catch from that. *(He goes to sit in his chair.)*

MEADOWS: Alright, just—don't sit. Stay…stay where you are. I'll be with you in a minute. *(Slight beat, half to himself.)* Oh this is silly.

(MEADOWS approaches TED. They hug. An awkward, mechanical hug. First MEADOWS taps TED on the back. Then TED taps MEADOWS on the back. They part. Beat)

MEADOWS: How about you give me a good punch in the face instead. I think you could put more feeling into that.

(Slight beat. Blackout)

Scene 7:
Heart

(Both MEADOWS *and* TED *clasp each other in a warm hug.)*

MEADOWS: Mmmm.

TED: Is this good?

MEADOWS: Mmmm… Good for you too?

TED: Yes. —Nice.

MEADOWS: Strange what a difference this makes. You think it wouldn't.

(Slight beat)

TED: I'd prefer if there were actual breasts pressing up against me.

MEADOWS: *(Laughs)* Agreed. That would be—well— that would be the cherry on the cake. —Or: "cherries".

TED: Yes.

MEADOWS: *(Slight beat)* I was making a crude joke.

TED: I got it.

MEADOWS: Nipples, you see.

TED: You don't have to explain it.

MEADOWS: Dance with me?

*(*TED *laughs.)*

TED: What?

MEADOWS: Come on, let's dance.

TED: …

MEADOWS: I'm serious.

TED: Dance with you?

MEADOWS: Why not. "Cut the rug." Or is it "cut up the rug"? Whatever the expression. *(He disengages from* TED *but still holds on to him.)* Come on.

TED: You mean…just—?

MEADOWS: Do you have something better to do?—Another engagement I don't know about?

TED: Um—well…

MEADOWS: It'll be fun. *(Gives him a playful tug.)* We could do with fun. Open the spigots. Let the fun pour out.

TED: Um. Well.

MEADOWS: It's not complicated. I'll lead you follow.

(MEADOWS attempts to dance with TED. TED resists.)

TED: Hold on. Wait a minute.

MEADOWS: A little jig. Look: we'll sway a little to start with, okay?

TED: I— *(Laughs)*

MEADOWS: Why not? Seriously.

TED: Well…

MEADOWS: You old fart. You are acting like an old fart.

TED: I—don't know.

MEADOWS: Why?

TED: Let's not…

MEADOWS: What?

TED: Push it. Let's not push it.

MEADOWS: Push what?

TED: *(A laugh)* You'll ask to sleep with me next. *(Slight beat)* I'm joking.

MEADOWS: I won't do that.

TED: I know.

MEADOWS: This is not the opening salvo for romance, Ted. I'm not plotting to screw you.

TED: I know, yes.

MEADOWS: I'm not building up to anything.

TED: I didn't think you were.

MEADOWS: My next request will not require we take our clothes off.

TED: Wonderful. *(Joking:)* I was worried.

MEADOWS: I don't find you the least bit attractive.

TED: What a relief.

(Slight beat)

MEADOWS: You have a way with emotions. Drives me up the wall.

TED: I don't dance. That's all. Never have.

MEADOWS: Have you ever swayed? From side to side? For enjoyment?

TED: I do that when I'm teaching—strangely. It's more of a nervous tick.

MEADOWS: With music? Ever swayed with music?

TED: We don't have music.

MEADOWS: I'll hum something.

TED: Not the same. We can't dance without music.

MEADOWS: You do it in class.

TED: By myself, yes. Like I said it's more of a nervous tick. Like a metronome. You can't talk about a metronome swaying, can you?

MEADOWS: You *are* a metronome.

TED: Well—precision counts.

MEADOWS: You're telling me you've never ever swayed with someone without music?

TED: It's not a rite of passage is it? It's not like it's *that* common.

MEADOWS: We'll make up a tune. You tick, I'll compose.

TED: It wouldn't be the same without real music.

MEADOWS: You have an imagination.

TED: Medcalf.

MEADOWS: MEADOWS! It's: MEADOWS! You know what? ...Why don't we just wait for a good percussion set to kick off when the bombs start falling. We're overdue for another round. If there's one thing you can depend on in these parts is things blowing up. And when it does, hey: we can do a tango to the tune of bombs blowing up civilians. Would that be music enough for you?

(TED *gives* MEADOWS *a look.*)

MEADOWS: What?

TED: ...

MEADOWS: What?!

TED: That's not funny.

MEADOWS: What isn't?

TED: What you just said. Sick.

MEADOWS: "Sick"?

TED: Yes.

MEADOWS: Me?

TED: Perverse.

MEADOWS: *What?*

TED: For all your talk of emotions and hugging and the rest of it, you don't have much heart, do you; when it comes down to it. Empathy for yourself, sure. Lots of feeling there, but not for anyone else. Not really.

MEADOWS: *(Stunned)* Oh. —That's—

TED: It's true. From the beginning. From the moment I knew you.

MEADOWS: That actually takes my breath away. I actually feel robbed of my next breath by that breathtaking thing you just said, just now.

TED: Well you don't.

MEADOWS: I don't. *I* don't? When I've spent these past—*four months* knocking myself out trying to get a twitch out of you.

TED: Is that what you've been doing?

MEADOWS: Yes. It's like I've been milking a dead fucking cow trying to get *any* kind of human response out of you.

TED: You've been milking a dead fucking cow?

MEADOWS: A dead fucking cow. The milk of human kindness is not a fluid you possess, my friend.

TED: Like you're overflowing with it; the way you care *so* much about those people out there who are suffering under *our* bombs.

MEADOWS: Excuse me while I care a little more about what's happening to us right here. When I'm safely back at home watching the nightly news *then* I'll have all the compassion in the world for the population from whose ranks our torturers come from!

TED: "Torturers." Because being forced to read a Winnie the Pooh cook book is such a mind fuck.

MEADOWS: Actually, yes, it is! And, as a side note, our liberty—having that taken away from us!

TED: You know what you've been doing this entire time?

MEADOWS: Wow. You're still shilling for them, even now.

TED: You've bullied me—

MEADOWS: Unbelievable.

TED: You've bullied me—

MEADOWS: Stockholm syndrome, that's what this is.

TED: What?

MEADOWS: If they came in and raped you you'd make excuses: "rape is an oppressed man's weapon against his Western oppressors!" You'll do a Patty Hearst next.

TED: Don't be disgusting.

MEADOWS: Wait, did you say "bullied" you?

TED: Yes! These past four months.

MEADOWS: Bullied you?

TED: With your pitiful—

MEADOWS: Are you kidding me?

TED: *(Overlapping)* —whining, and—

MEADOWS: Bullying *you?*

TED: —badgering me, twenty-four hours, with your— nauseating—!

MEADOWS: Me?!

TED: Self pity, and woe is me—

MEADOWS: What are you talking about ?

TED: *(Overlapping; mocking whiny voice.)* "Why me? why me?"

MEADOWS: Come again. What the fuck. Are you kidding me?

TED: *(Overlapping)* Going around with your hands out, begging for attention.

MEADOWS: *Begging?*

TED: Flapping about like a prima donna with a thorn in her pinkie.

MEADOWS: Wait a minute, hold on.

TED: "Give me a hug; give me a massage; can I feel your leg? can I feel your scar? dance with me, Ted, make it better, Ted."

MEADOWS: *(Overlapping)* Excuse me. —Excuse me.

TED: *(Overlapping)* On a loop, over and over, Jesus Christ.

MEADOWS: This isn't a cocktail party. This isn't—this isn't a faculty soiree. I'm not at a meet-and-greet, I can't leave. I ran out of sparkling conversation the minute they put a hood over my head. I think I might be excused for being a little self-centered, or surly; or bringing out the old violin and striking up a dirge and make like I'm dying *because I am*. Perverse? You have the gall to call *me* perverse? I'M A FUCKING HOSTAGE! There's no such animal as a perverse hostage!

(TED moves away from MEADOWS.)

MEADOWS: And what's this about "not much heart"? I'm the only one around here who has a functioning heart. "I've not much heart"! Tell me I'm short on balls, I'll consider that, but heart, I've got fucking heart. The only one in working condition for miles around. Have a listen. Listen to it, Ted, you might learn how a real one sounds.

(MEADOWS grabs TED's neck in an effort to pull him towards his chest.)

TED: Fuck off!

(TED pushes MEADOWS away.)

MEADOWS: You're the one with the problem. You're the one with a fucking metronome in *here*. *(Points to his heart)*

TED: Here's the thing: —I don't want to dance with you. I just—don't. I'm sorry. I've tried. I mean—I have *really* tried. But I still don't like you. Close—a couple of times. But I can always depend on you to remind me of why you are fundamentally an *asshat*. A dyed-in-the-wool, reactionary, piece of shit. And we can't do a tango to the tune of bombs blowing up civilians even if we wanted to because our countrymen, fortunately, have taken a break from bombing the living daylights out of this city.

MEADOWS: Oh, come on. We won't let a minor consideration like that get in our way. We'll ask our hosts to do something to provoke a response, you know, down a plane, kill off a few innocents abroad. Or we can just ask them to strike up a skirmish right here. Gunfire has a great musical beat. We'll ask them to fire off some rounds just for us. *(He moves to the door.)* Hey! Fellas! Give us a skirmish we can dance to!

TED: *(Overlapping last sentence)* Shut up. Shut the fuck up. Shut up!

(TED forcibly moves MEADOWS away from the door.)

MEADOWS: That's right. Hit me. Go ahead. If I can't have a dance, a punch will be swell. That and the hug, last me for days.

(TED breaks away from MEADOWS.)

MEADOWS: Sick? Yes. I'm a little under-the-weather. Not doing so great. I'm feeling a little needy. I apologize for that but my needs aren't being met, you see. I feel like I'm disappearing a little bit every day. Melting into the woodwork. I don't have your political backbone; your righteous delusions to see me through this shit. If all you can offer is a good punch, if that's all you can give after reaching deep down into yourself and finding nothing but that, I'll take it. Punch away. It wouldn't be the same if I did it to myself. *(Hits himself in the stomach)* See? It's not the same. *(Hits himself)* It's not the same. Or this: *(Slaps his face this time)* Not: *(Slap)* Not: *(Slap)* Not the same. Poor substitute for the real thing. It has to come from someone else, you see. That way I won't feel so fucking alone all the time. *(Slight beat)* What I wouldn't give for twenty-four hours of non-stop bombing just to spite you… Dear God…dear God: bring on the fucking slaughter.

(Slight beat. Blackout. In the blackout, sounds of bombs falling.)

Scene 8:
One more story before bedtime

(Sounds of gunfire and bombs exploding in the distance. In spite of the noise they can still hear each other without having to raise their voices… Dim lighting. Perhaps periodic flashes from the bombs and flames flare in through the cracks… TED picks up a deck chair and hurls it across the room. He picks up the other deck chair and does the same… He picks it up yet again and throws it across the room. MEADOWS watches impassively.)

(The door opens. A GUARD enters. He stops in the doorway. He looks at the deck chairs… He picks one up, puts the bar in its groove, and sets it down. He does the same with the other chair… He remains standing by the chair, looking at TED.)

TED: You know—I could really use a drink right about now. *(Slight beat)* Scotch. Ice. —Not too much ice. Two cubes. Heavy on the scotch. *(Slight beat, to MEADOWS)* Now if you were a bottle of scotch, I'd dance with you.

(Slight beat)

MEADOWS: If I was a bottle of scotch, I'd dance with myself. —Who'd need you if I had that.

(The GUARD holds out his arms offering to dance. Slight beat)

TED: Not you.

(The GUARD continues to offer.)

TED: Scotch.

GUARD: …

TED: Drink?

GUARD: *(Points skyward; accent:)* Bombs. Shops close. No selling… You want to dance?

MEADOWS: I'm next in line. Take a number.

(The GUARD looks at MEADOWS.)

It's called waiting your turn. —Ever heard of fair play? Or is that too Western a concept for you?

MEADOWS: Your country drop bombs on us… We have no weapon to fight this. Is this what you mean by fair play? —What they do now?

MEADOWS: We have nothing to do with that.

GUARD: No?

MEADOWS: Obviously not. We're here. We're stuck here; we're not in those planes. *(Slight beat)* Anyway… if Ted's dancing with anyone, it's me.

TED: I'd prefer a drink.

MEADOWS: Yes. But…should there be dancing.

TED: *(Disagreeing:)* Well…

(Slight beat)

MEADOWS: Why am I not surprised. Dancing with the enemy, literally. Of course.

TED: I didn't say that. I'm just saying—I wouldn't be so presumptuous.

MEADOWS: Really? You'd choose him over me?

TED: I didn't say that either.

MEADOWS: And just to be clear…it would be my personality, not my looks, that would put you off? Right?

TED: *(Slight beat)* Again… um…

MEADOWS: Can I just say, *(To the* GUARD*)* with you as my witness: *(To* TED*)* Fuck off.

GUARD: You two are funny.

MEADOWS: Yes, well—we're playing this gig for the foreseeable future. Right? So—drop in anytime.

GUARD: One of these bombs from your planes fell on my building tonight… My sister was home…making dinner. *(Slight beat)* Now…you can't see what is dinner…and what is her. *(Slight beat, to* TED*)* You want a drink? *(Slight beat)* I will get you a drink.

(The GUARD *exits. Silence between* MEADOWS *and* TED. *The occasional muffled sounds of explosions, gunfire.)*

MEADOWS: I've grown fond of the name Medcalf.

TED: I'm sorry to hear that. —He was a colleague I detested, at another university. Taught computers… Entitled little brat.

MEADOWS: *(Slight beat)* Not someone you'd want to be stuck with on a desert island.

TED: Not someone I'd want to die with, no. *(Slight beat)* He's a huge success in his field now… Living the life. Condos, cars…

MEADOWS: *(Slight beat)* Well even I detest him now.

TED: To think you can be so bright in one area. And a dumb ass in everything else.

MEADOWS: Nature's way of of not putting everything in one basket. I'm guessing.

TED: Is that what it is.

MEADOWS: I should've gone into computers… Fiddled with bits and bytes instead of verbs and nouns. —What god-awful choices I've made. Really… The joke is I thought teaching abroad might be a cure-all. A spa for a mid-life crisis. Break out of my habits, routines. Take control. Get re-acquainted with my—what? Man—, manliness? …Everyone around me seemed to have so much more—passion. You know? When you think everyone else knows where they're going except you. So: travel. Isn't that what some people do when they feel—lost? Go on an adventure to find themselves. Meet new kinds of people. Understand other points of views. Sleep with other kinds of people. Then return home with a better…a better something. Understanding—of themselves. And…other stuff.

(Slight beat)

TED: You still might. —It's not over.

MEADOWS: *(Slight beat)* I thought these kinds of experiences were supposed to—if not free of shit at least be—positive—by the end. —The travel books I read were in the self-help section. The How-To-Be-A-Better-You shelf.

(Slight beat)

TED: Like I said, it's not over yet.

(Beat)

MEADOWS: Can I come over to where you are? …I promise I won't ask for a hug. Or a dance, or anything.

(Slight beat)

TED: As it happens, there's no one else vying for this spot next to me. It's wide open, so…

(Slight beat)

MEADOWS: Can I get you anything from this side of the room?

TED: No. Thank you.

(Slight beat)

MEADOWS: Nothing at all?

TED: What've you got?

MEADOWS: An apology?

TED: Don't bother. —Or I'll have to apologize next. And I don't want to do that.

MEADOWS: God forbid. *(Slight beat)* Well…I'll come over then. *(Slight beat; half to himself)* In a minute.

*(*MEADOWS *doesn't move. More sounds of bombing and gun fire. Beat)*

TED: Do you remember Mr Singh?

MEADOWS: Only what happened to him.

TED: The week before Mr Singh was killed…we'd gotten plastered… We'd gathered in the basement of our building… The city was getting hit hard. Heavy duty firefights; bombing. I'd run out and bought two bottles of scotch. My bit of bravery for the group. *(Absent, mocking)* My bit of bravery…Barbara, Bryan. Randa, Eva. And Mrs Singh. She'd come down to keep us company. *(Slight beat)* We all adored Mrs Singh. Earth mother if there ever was one. Always the hostess whatever the occasion. Never let the conversation flag. I think she knew we needed her. Even more than the scotch. She was always so…unruffled. *(Slight beat)* Mr Singh was still correcting papers in their top-floor apartment. "Upstairs with his religious faith for protection," she said. We all had a nervous laugh about that—even Mrs Singh. "My husband is not burdened with political convictions," she said. "But he does have his faith. His faith is his steel umbrella. Even on a night like this." *(Slight beat)* Some time later when the bombing had slowed—but not stopped, Mr Singh called down from the top of the stairs: "You must come up now, Mrs Singh." She looked up the stairwell and said: "Just one more bomb before bedtime, dear". *(Fondly remembering.)* "Just one more bomb before bedtime." She said that. *(Slight beat)* The next bomb eventually fell a few blocks away and she went to bed. *(Slight beat)* He'd become an American citizen only the year before...before he was kidnapped.

(Silence between MEADOWS *and* TED. TED *turns to* MEADOWS.*)*

TED: Are you telling me...you couldn't get laid once? In all this time. Not once?

(Slight beat)

MEADOWS: This country's been one big tease.

(The GUARD *enters. Draped on his shoulders are leg chains. He carries a glass. He walks over to* TED. *The* GUARD *hands the chains to* TED.*)*

GUARD: You will please put these on. Attach your legs to the radiator. *(To* MEADOWS*)* Please.

(Beat. MEADOWS *walks to the radiator.* TED *holds onto the chains. To* TED:*)*

GUARD: Now. You will do it now, please?

*(*TED *doesn't move.)*

GUARD: I am asking nicely.

(Beat. TED *passes a chain to* MEADOWS.*)*

GUARD: To the radiator.

MEADOWS: *(Looks at the chain)* All relative, I suppose. More freedom than a broom closet.

(MEADOWS *bends down and chains one of his legs to the radiator. After a beat,* TED *does the same thing reluctantly.*)

GUARD: *(To* TED*)* I brought you your drink... No electricity. No ice. *(Slight beat)* It is strange what you find in shops during war. I find no bread. No milk. But lots of bottles of soda water. So I mix some in to give the drink fizz. *(Slight beat)* You must be clever with rations during war. My sister was this way... What she do with very little...it always surprise me. They say it is more than ingredients that give a meal taste. It is the love you put in as well, yes? *(He offers the drink to* TED.*)* Your drink.

(TED *looks at the* GUARD; *at the drink.*)

MEADOWS: You could've brought me one.

GUARD: I wanted to. But my bladder could only fill one glass. If you are patient, I will return with another. *(Slight beat)* Your drink.

MEADOWS: You're... kidding.

GUARD: I'm a vegetarian. No toxic stuff.

(Slight beat)

MEADOWS: You're not kidding... You little fuck.

(The GUARD *looks at* MEADOWS.*)*

MEADOWS: Look...we're really sorry about your sister. I've a sister myself. I'd be pissed, no, more than pissed, I'd go fucking ballistic. But for God's sake, look at us. We're not exactly the world's decision makers here. We don't give orders or push buttons, we don't drop bombs. We have nothing to do with this!

GUARD: You cheer your team when they score a goal, yes? You wave the flag, you cheer your troops.

MEADOWS: Not me. I don't.

GUARD: And after you cheer you switch off TV and forget. You forget what has been done. For you. In your name.

MEADOWS: Not in mine; we have nothing to do with this.

GUARD: And my sister? What did she have to do with it?

MEADOWS: We're not responsible! You can't—you can't hold us accountable. Seriously, our—condolences, but it can't be this random, it can't. You might as well round up all the penguins in Antarctica. They're about as much to blame for your sister's death as we are.

GUARD: I think these penguins you talk of are a little more innocent than you.

(TED *interrupts by taking the drink from the* GUARD.)

TED: About the door. The day it was left open… Were we meant to escape? *(Beat)* Ah… Huh. *(Slight beat. Toasts with the drink)* To the memory of your sister.

GUARD: To your health.

TED: I'll drink to that.

(TED *drinks, emptying the glass.* MEADOWS *winces. Slight beat.* TED *hands the glass back to the* GUARD. *The* GUARD *takes out an envelope from his pocket and hands it to* TED. *Silence between the three)*

TED: Letter from home?

GUARD: If you believe in God…perhaps. Perhaps, yes. A way to get home.

(Slight beat)

TED: *(To* GUARD*)* What will you do now?

GUARD: I will bury more of my family today… And then I will learn to cook for myself.

TED: *(Remembering:)* Oh. Then... *(Picks up the nearby Winnie-the-Pooh cook book.)* ...you'll be wanting this. There are some decent recipes in here. Made me want to try some out myself.

(TED hands the GUARD the book.)

GUARD: I have forgotten this book... This was my sister's... Thank you.

TED: You're welcome.

(Slight beat. Blackout)

Scene 9:
The envelope, please.

(MEADOWS and TED on stage as before, their legs chained to the radiator. The GUARD has exited. The envelope lies at Ted's feet. He holds two straws, one shorter than the other. The battle outside has died down. Silence between the two)

MEADOWS: That is so offensive... That it's come down to this. —So...so offensive, really. Just a horrible lack of imagination. Like we're some party game for them. *(Slight beat)* You're the expert here. Work it out with them. —Kiss their behinds. Tell them how much you believe in their cause or something. Tell them how much I've fought for oppressed people all my life. Lie, yes. Sell it. Make them understand we're not the enemy. Get them to see we're just two working stiffs with the worst fucking luck in the world.

(TED holds out the two straws to MEADOWS. Shakes his head.)

MEADOWS: No.

(TED still holds them out. MEADOWS shakes his head.)

MEADOWS: No. —I'm not playing. I won't.

TED: Pick one.

MEADOWS: No.

TED: Just pick one.

MEADOWS: Don't have to. Won't do it. Nope. Not playing.

(TED *holds one straw in each hand.*)

TED: Do you want this one? Or this one? It makes no difference. We don't know which one means what. The short straw could be the winning straw. You know how they like to fuck with us.

(Slight beat)

MEADOWS: I've a wife. *(Slight beat)* Yes, I was going to cheat on her. But I still have one. Who loves me. Who'd be heartbroken. And my mother. It would kill my mother.

TED: Choose… For once in your life. Do something brave.

MEADOWS: *(Almost in tears)* I am! I'm choosing not to play. I'm saying fuck you. To them. —We need to stand up to them. Neither of us asked to be in this thing. I certainly didn't; maybe you did, but I did not.

(TED, *holding out the two straws, approaches* MEADOWS. MEADOWS *backs away.*)

MEADOWS: No.

(TED *continues to approach.* MEADOWS *backs away.*)

MEADOWS: No. I told you. I'm not playing, I don't want to. Stop moving.

(MEADOWS *trips at the end of his chain, ending on his backside.*)

MEADOWS: Please.

(*Beat.* MEADOWS *lies flat on his back.* TED *approaches, stands over him. He bends down. And places the longer straw on* MEADOWS's *chest. He remains crouching over him for a moment. Then straightens up. He looks at the straw. Twiddles it about.)*

TED: First I put up with you all these months. And now this… This really is the last straw.

*(*TED *chuckles at his own joke. He quietly chuckles some more, really taken by his own humor, and the fact that he's able to laugh.* MEADOWS *doesn't laugh. It dies down. Beat)*

TED: Well I thought it was funny.

(Slight beat. Blackout. The sound of a gun firing once.)

END OF PLAY

www.ingramcontent.com/pod-product-compliance
Lightning Source LLC
Chambersburg PA
CBHW070030110426
42741CB00035B/2709